Around the World in 72 Days

Contents

Written by Liz Miles

Illustrated by Monica Auriemma
and Martin Sanders

Collins

Nellie Bly's adventure

Nellie Bly was born in the United States of America in 1864. She became a reporter.

In Nellie's time, travel was tricky and slow.

Nellie read a story in which a man travelled around the world in 80 days.

4

She dared herself to complete this trip in 70 days, in a real-life adventure.

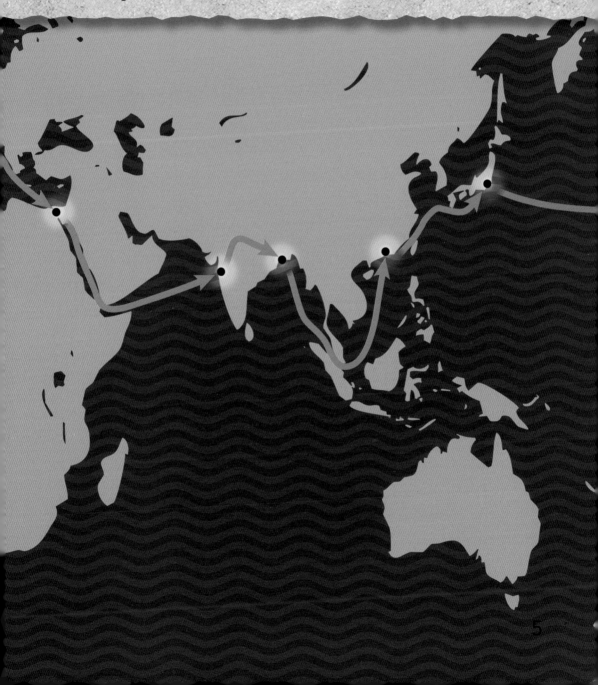

Departure

Nellie's boss said she needed a chaperone
(a person going with her to keep her safe), but
Nellie went alone. She just took a small satchel.

Nellie's departure was at 9:40 a.m. on 14 November 1889.

The adventure began on a steamship.
There were no planes then.

9

Nellie was unlucky on her departure. She got seasick!

People wondered whether Nellie would be up to the adventure. Would she survive disease, fever and storms?

Speed

To hit the 70-day target, Nellie had to catch ships and trains on time.

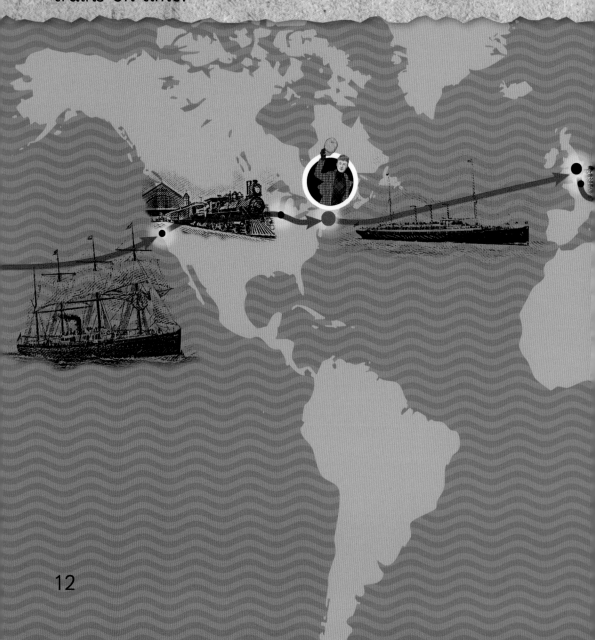

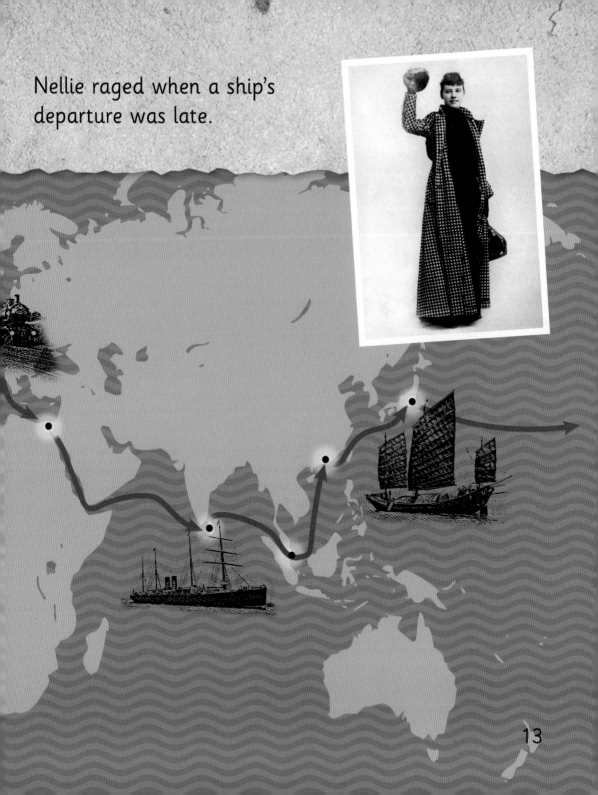

Nellie raged when a ship's departure was late.

While waiting for ships, she reported on nature and festive events.

She battled with rainy days and even storms.

Nellie was pleased when she got midway round the world and reached Hong Kong. She was two days ahead at this stage!

But then she was unlucky. Her ship to Japan was five days late.

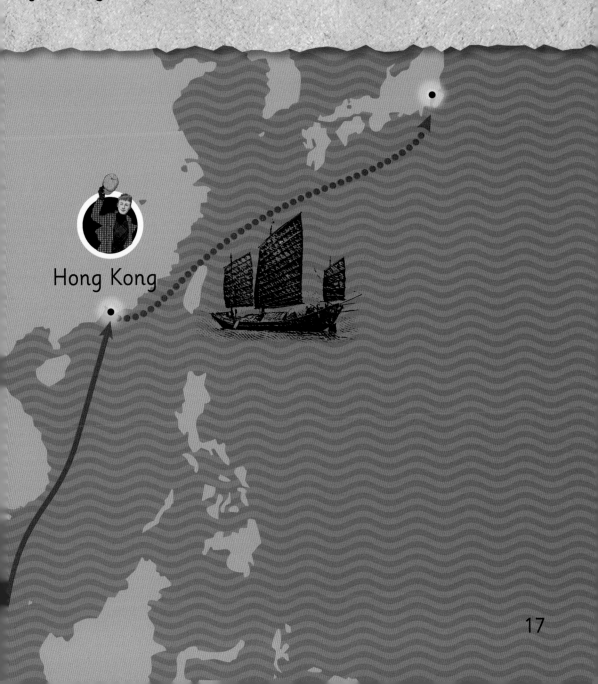

Hong Kong

On 7 January, Nellie had just 25 days to battle across 8000 miles of sea.

When she arrived on land, there was a terrible snowstorm. This meant Nellie had to catch a different train to complete her trip.

Triumphant

Nellie completed the adventure in 72 days, setting a world record for travelling around the Earth.

She put the key stages of her adventure in a book.
Her story still inspires people today.

Nellie's trip

Day 1:
14 November 1889,
United States

Day 72:
25 January 1890,
United States

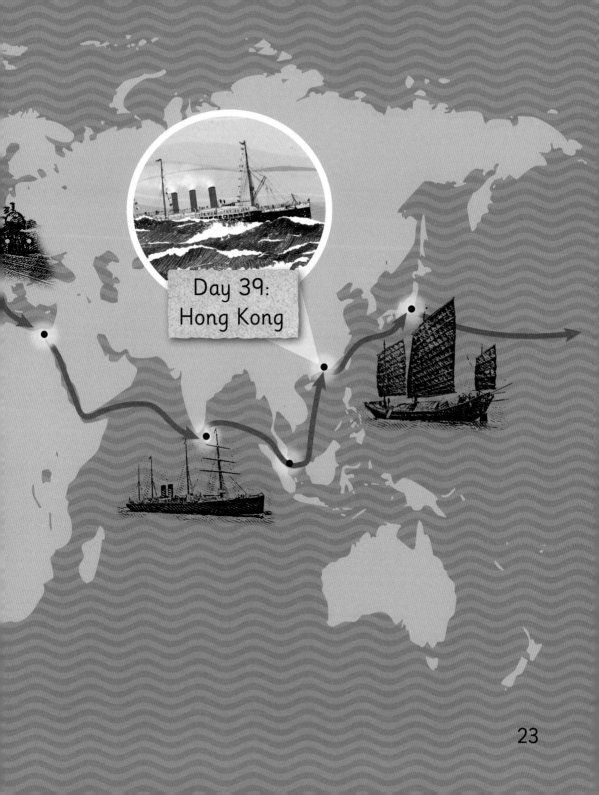

Day 39:
Hong Kong

🐾 Review: After reading 🐾

Use your assessment from hearing the children read to choose any GPCs, words or tricky words that need additional practice.

Read 1: Decoding

- Help the children to get quicker at reading multi-syllable words. Look at the following words: exactly   slippery   adventure
- Ask the children to:
  - Sound talk and blend each syllable "chunk".
  - Then read each chunk in turn.
  - Now read the whole word quickly.

Read 2: Prosody

- Choose two double page spreads and model reading with expression to the children. Ask the children to have a go at reading the same pages with expression.
- Tell the children you are going to read pages 8–9 as if you are a radio reporter, telling an audience about the beginning of Nellie's great adventure. Use your voice to create excitement.
- Ask the children to read a page in the same manner.

Read 3: Comprehension

- Turn to pages 22 and 23 and recap the journey Nellie took on her trip around the world.
- For every question ask the children how they know the answer. Ask:
  - What job did Nellie do? (*she was a reporter*)
  - What did Nellie aim to do? (*travel around the world in 70 days*)
  - What were some of the difficulties Nellie faced on her trip? (e.g. *the weather, she got seasick, sometimes ships were late*)
- What sort of a person do you think Nellie was? Why?